LARA BOYD trained at Glas
Technology and Glasgow
a qualified Trainer and Assessor working as a training
Consultant mainly in the field of health promotion.

Since *First Foods Fast* was first published in 2002
Lara has been delivering a training programme which
she wrote and developed for NHS Lanarkshire, based
on her book. Now entitled 'Lanarkshire Healthy
Weaning Initiative' and first piloted by Healthy Valleys:
the Healthy Living Initiative, Lara has worked with
parents and their Health Visitors across the region.
She is invited to talk about *First Foods Fast* at
seminars and workshops and also develops other
training programmes in the field of health promotion
and cookery for Healthy Valleys, aimed at children and
families.

Lara is married to Jamie and they have three gorgeous
boys, James, Robert and Scott, who all have big
appetites for good food – most of the time!

CINDERS MCLEOD, cartoonist and illustrator, worked in
Glasgow for many years, where her cartoons of
'Broomie Law' appeared in *The Herald* newspaper.
She now lives in Canada, working for the *Toronto
Globe and Mail*. She is intrigued by the way children
see the world, and her own two constantly provide
inspiration.

First Foods Fast

How to prepare delicious simple meals for
your baby, from first tastes to one year

LARA BOYD

Luath Press Limited

EDINBURGH

www.luath.co.uk

First Published 2002
This edition 2007

ISBN (10): 1-905222-46-7
ISBN (13): 978-1-9-0522246-9

The recipe suggestions included in this book have been carefully researched and tested. The author and publishers can accept no responsibility for any accident, loss, illness or inconvenience arising.

The paper used in this book is recyclable. It is made from low-chlorine pulps produced in a low-emission manner from renewable forests.

Printed in the UK by
CPI Bookmarque, Croydon, CR0 4TD

Designed by Tom Bee

Typeset in 11 point Meta

Illustrations by Cinders McLeod

Contents

Foreword

Solid food can wait. Be in no hurry to move your baby on to foods and feasting. When the time comes, start slowly. Give your baby a chance to enjoy feeling food in their mouth, let them spit, splash and play with it. Soon they will swallow and start on their own personal journey to the delights of a grown up diet. *First Foods Fast* shows you how to keep food basic and simple remembering that infants take a while to develop and get used to new tastes. Give them time and enjoy the slow, reflective, exploratory way that infants learn about food.

Simple, basic ingredients and minimal preparation and skills are the key ingredients for preparing healthy foods for healthy children. *First Foods Fast* provides all the essential ingredients to help nurture the new person at the table. Three course meals can wait – start by focusing on simple ingredients and good taste for a lifetime. Enjoy the simple pleasures of feeding your baby well!

Annie S. Anderson BSc PhD SRD
Professor of Food Choice,
Centre for Public Health Nutrition Research,
Ninewells Medical School,
University of Dundee

Annie is also an expert member of the Scientific Advisory Committee on Nutrition, Maternal and Child Nutrition Sub-group

Introduction

A great deal has happened since *First Foods Fast* was first published in 2002. I now have three boys with whom I can share my love of food and cooking and who were all weaned straight onto freshly prepared food. I developed a training workshop based on *First Foods Fast* and have had the immense privilege of meeting many parents and their Health Visitors who are determined to provide the best possible start for their babies.

I have learned a great deal from everyone I've worked with and believe, now more than ever, that tasting a new food or meal should be an exciting prospect and not something a child learns to dread.

Starting out as you mean to go on is definitely easier on everyone. It is simpler for the parent who doesn't have to backtrack their child from a range of bad eating habits. Parents should encourage their baby to be interested in real food and become aware of its appearance, texture and taste. This is easier on the baby who is very gradually introduced to new foods and tastes, until finally he or she is old enough to eat with the whole family.

First Foods Fast is still intended to be a simple and easy to use kitchen tool: an instant solution for those sometimes difficult, sometimes sleep deprived months of your baby's first year. This new book has been expanded to include some new recipes and a new section on finger foods and contains over 40 different suggestions and recipe ideas. I hope I can continue to dispel the myth that cooking for your baby is difficult, time consuming or expensive and provide inspiration for your own ideas for the very first stages of weaning your baby.

Lara Boyd

Suggestions for preparing the recipes

All the recipes in this book are made with simple fresh ingredients which are easy to buy. You don't have to buy expensive food items to feed your baby well, in fact the simpler the better because then you can personally control key elements of your baby's diet, for instance low salt and sugar intake. None of the recipes require you to add any salt or sugar and you should not substitute any 'cook in' type sauces or gravy for the fresh ingredients suggested as these can contain high levels of both. Some of the recipes ask for canned ingredients, for instance canned beans, lentils, fish etc. – where possible always try to use a product which does not contain salt in the ingredients list. It is worth remembering that products canned in oil or water will contain less salt than products canned in brine as the word brine simply means 'salt water'. In addition, where a recipe asks for bread, do not use soda bread which contains more salt than ordinary bread. Some babies can have a pre-disposition to a food allergy of one kind or other; if this concerns you then please speak with your Health Visitor or doctor before using the recipes in this book.

The recipes are divided into two sections. The recipes

in the first section, 'First Tastes', are suitable for infants during the very first stage of weaning. Some ingredients are not suitable for babies under 6 months e.g. cow's milk products. This is when you are introducing your baby to solid foods for the very first time and breast or formula milk is still being offered as usual. The flavours need not be mild and the texture you first feed your baby can be a completely smooth paste or purée to complement the liquid diet your baby has been receiving until now. Try offering a very small amount after a milk feed or in the middle of one. Your baby's appetite will dictate how fast or slow this first stage of weaning progresses – never force food onto an unreceptive baby.

The recipes in the second section, 'Introducing New Tastes and Variety', are suitable for those babies who have moved on from a completely smooth purée and are also eating solid food regularly. Some ingredients in the second section, like wheat flour, egg and cow's milk are not suitable for babies under 6 months. There is a greater variety of flavours in this section and initially the texture will be a slightly thicker purée. Once your baby is used to eating solid food you can simply adapt the methods suggested in each recipe to retain some of the natural lumps and texture of the foods. I found it best to do this very gradually, allowing your baby to go at his or her own pace, exploring their food. Allow your baby to touch their food if they wish and gradually they may start to feed themselves with their fingers.

I have not suggested any recipe ideas for breakfast because you may have a personal preference. As your baby starts to eat three meals a day you can offer a mixed breakfast of cereal and fruit or yoghurt, whatever is most suitable for your baby and fits easily into your daily routine. Always seek advice if you are unsure of what to give.

I have given an approximate cooking time with each dish to help you plan for meal times and to give an idea of which meals are quicker to make when you're in a hurry. However it is important that no one single meal is given repeatedly as the aim is to introduce your baby to lots of different tastes and textures and in doing so provide a well balanced diet of vitamins, minerals, carbohydrates, proteins and fats. However, if you are in a hurry, make the dish thicker than your baby normally likes and then once you have placed the mixture in a bowl for feeding you can add more milk (if cooking for a baby over 6 months) or water to thin it out and cool it down at the same time. You won't have to wait so long for the food to cool to the right temperature and, let's face it, when you've got a baby crying for his or her next meal, seconds do count! This tip applies to any of the recipes in this book, even those which don't originally call for milk. Where vegetables have to be boiled you can also use a microwave to help reduce the cooking times, but never be tempted to give your baby food straight from the microwave.

The food may have hot spots which could burn the inside of your baby's mouth, so stir it well and then test it. You should always test the tempera-ture of any food before you give it to your baby – it should be cool enough to place a small amount on the back of your own hand.

The way in which we cook food for ourselves as well as for our babies is very important. This is because some of the nutrient content can be lost through poor cook-ing methods. For instance, when cooking vegetables in water, nutrients are lost into the water, and if the water is drained away and discarded, nutrients will be thrown away at the same time. Try using less water than usual so that the vegetables absorb the water as they cook and you can then add what little water may be left to the dish. The quantity of vegetables asked for in these recipes is very small so I found that approximately 150 ml of plain unsalted water was enough to cook the vegetables but still leave them moist and tender.

Each recipe makes approximately 150 g (5 oz) of food but different babies have larger or smaller appetites, so you may have to increase or decrease the amounts given. Once you have tried a few of the recipes for yourself you will have a better idea of how much food to make up. Always introduce any new food gradually, giving a tiny amount at first, your baby may only take one or two teaspoons of a new food as they learn to accept a new taste or texture. If your baby doesn't seem interested in a new food, don't press it on them – you can offer the same recipe again on another day.

Once you have made the dish it must either be eaten as soon as it is cool enough or refrigerated, but never keep any cooked, refrigerated food for longer than 24 hours as it will start to spoil and may go off. If your baby does not finish the whole meal don't keep any left-overs. If you are making up meals in advance and then freezing them, be sure never to keep any frozen food for longer than three months as there are some nasty bugs which can survive the freezing process and the food will spoil, so you will find it useful to date anything you freeze.

If prepared and frozen properly, whether you are making up baby recipes or adapting your own home cooked food, it does not take long to build up a good stock of delicious, healthy fast foods.

Even if you're a new mother or father who's never cooked before, you should find my recipes easy to prepare. The suggested variations which follow most of the recipes will expand the number of possible dishes you can try even further.

First Tastes

Please check the ingredients in this section are suitable for your baby e.g. cow's milk products. Refer to page 11 and seek advice from your Health Visitor or GP if you are unsure.

Rice with Milk

'Baby Rice', as the food processing companies call it, is generally accepted as one of the first foods used to introduce your baby to solid foods and food in general. It has a mild creamy taste and is low in fibre, which is important when switching from a liquid diet. Some manufacturers add vitamins and minerals to their 'Baby Rice' and some don't, so always check the ingredients list to see what you are paying for. However, you can buy ordinary rice which is ground up and therefore just as easy to use as the 'Baby Rice', not to mention much cheaper to buy and I have suggested mixing it with breast milk or infant formula to provide those added vitamins and minerals. You won't find ground rice in the baby food section of your supermarket, so

*you may have to ask which section it is shelved in –
normally the baking aisle next to pudding rice. This
first taste dish is so easy to make that I decanted
some ground rice into a little airtight plastic box and
added it to the bag of tricks, which every parent finds
themselves carrying around with the baby, just in case I
found myself somewhere other than at home over a
meal time. If you are giving your baby solid food for the
very first time you may want to make up less than the
amounts given – just follow the suggestions below.*

Approximate cooking time: 4 minutes

Ingredients

1 tablespoon ground rice

150 ml breast milk or infant formula milk

Method

Note: If you want to make less than 5 oz of food then
simply reduce the amounts of each ingredient in equal
proportion. If you are introducing your baby to solids
for the very first time then start by using just 1 or 2
teaspoons of ground rice and gradually add a very
small amount of milk. Be guided by the consistency of
the mixture to tell you if you need more or less fluid.
With trial and error you can make up as much or as
little as you like.

1. Place the milk in a small metal saucepan, add the
   rice and stir it into the milk.

2. Leave to cook, over a moderate heat, but watch it carefully, because you don't want it to boil.

3. When the mixture first starts to bubble, turn the heat down slightly and stir continuously. The dish is ready when the mixture is thick and gloopy.

4. When you have achieved the consistency you require, turn the mixture out into a bowl for feeding and allow to cool.

5. Always stir and then check the temperature before feeding any hot food to your baby.

Creamed Potato

If you wish, use a smaller amount of potato at first with more milk, but you will be surprised how sweet the potato tastes in the quantities given.

Approximate cooking time: 14 minutes

Ingredients

1 small to medium potato

125 ml breast milk or infant formula

Method

1. Peel and wash the potato.

2. Chop it up into small cubes for faster cooking.

3. Place the pieces into a small metal pan and pour in approximately 150 ml of plain unsalted water. Cover the pan with a lid and leave to cook over a moderate to high heat. Do check the water level occasionally, and if the water is all absorbed by the potato before it is cooked then just add a little more to finish cooking.

4. When the potato is soft enough to break with the side of a fork, add the milk to the pan and mash the ingredients together.

5. Then either blend the mixture or mash any remaining lumps out with the back of a fork until you have the required consistency.

6. Turn the mixture out into a bowl for feeding and allow to cool.

7. Stir and then check the temperature before feeding to your baby.

Variations

Try creaming other vegetables in the same way. e.g. parsnip or turnip. Sweet potato is also a delicious alternative and even quicker to cook. You can also mix different vegetables together to increase variety – try mixing potato and broccoli florets together.

Stewed Fruit

It's great to get children into the habit of eating fruit from the earliest possible stage. There are a number of fruits which you can cook to enable your baby to taste them right from the start, and which make a great 'packed lunch' if you are on the move, but always remember to remove any skin, core and pips or stones.

Approximate Cooking time: 6 minutes

Ingredients

1 eating apple – Cox's Pippin, Golden Delicious or just ask your grocer for a sweeter variety of eating apple

2 tablespoons water

Method

1. Wash and peel the apple.

2. Cut the apple into four sections, lengthways, from top to bottom and remove all visible core and pips.

3. Slice the four pieces thinly.

4. Place the apple in a small metal saucepan with the water, cook over a high heat, stirring occasionally, and cover the pan with a lid for faster cooking.

5. After 3 minutes check that the apple is soft enough to mash with a fork. If it needs further cooking turn the heat down or it may burn.

6. Once the apple is soft, place in a bowl and mash

with the back of a fork until you have the consistency you require for feeding.

7. Turn the mixture out into a bowl for feeding and allow to cool.

8. Stir and then check the temperature before serving to your baby.

Variations

Try stewing pear, nectarines or peach. If they are ripe these fruit will take less time to cook than an apple. Your baby will also enjoy melon or banana which can be mashed without cooking, but again, always watch out for pips and skin and be careful not to offer banana which is still green as it will not mash as easily and will not be as sweet to taste.

Puréed Carrot

Carrot is an ideal vegetable to give your baby as a first taste because it is so good for you, but it is also naturally sweet tasting, after a diet of sweet milk. Do remember, however, to alternate it with the other first taste recipes, as it is possible to eat more carrot than is good for your baby.

Approximate cooking time: 14 minutes

Ingredients

140 g carrot
150 ml boiled water, cooled

Method

1. Peel and wash the carrot.

2. Chop it into very small pieces for faster cooking and place into a small metal pan.

3. Pour in approximately 150 ml of unsalted water and cover the pan with a lid, leave to cook over a moderate to high heat. Do check the water level occasionally, if the water is all absorbed by the carrot before it is cooked then just add a little more to finish cooking.

4. You can then either blend the carrot or mash it with the back of a fork until you have the required consistency.

5. Add some cooled boiled water if your baby finds the taste too strong at first.

6. Turn the carrot out into a bowl for feeding and allow to cool.

7. Stir and then check the temperature before feeding to your baby.

Variations

Try creaming other vegetables in the same way.

Cheese Sauce

This is another popular first taste dish. I have made the sauce using ground rice for quickness. If you are not used to making sauces it will help build confidence, because ground rice is so easy to use.

Approximate Cooking Time: 5 minutes

Ingredients

50 g mild white cheddar cheese

125 ml breast milk or infant formula

1 dessertspoon ground rice

Method

1. Grate the cheese.

2. Put the rice and milk into a small metal saucepan and stir together.

3. Add the cheese to the milk mixture and cook over a moderate heat, stirring continuously.

4. When the cheese has melted, turn the heat down and continue stirring until you have the consistency you require.

5. Turn the mixture into a bowl for feeding and allow to cool.

6. Stir and check the temperature before serving to your baby.

Variations

You could add ground herbs to increase or vary the flavour and try experimenting with other low salt cheeses.

Puréed Haricot Beans

Haricot beans are a good source of iron and protein and their flavour is so mild and creamy they make an excellent first taste dish. You can pre-cook your own dried beans very easily by soaking them overnight and then boiling them for at least 30 minutes until soft, but if you choose canned beans be sure you are buying a product which does not contain added salt, e.g. brine. Most varieties will give this information quite clearly on the label, but if in doubt leave it out.

Approximate Cooking Time: 7 minutes

Ingredients

85 g cooked or canned haricot beans

100 ml unsalted water

Method

1. Wash the beans.

2. Place them in a small metal saucepan with the water and start to cook over a moderate heat.

3. Once the water starts to bubble turn the heat down and stir continuously until the beans are soft enough to break up easily.

4. Turn the mixture out into a bowl for feeding and allow to cool.

5. Remove any skins and if there are still lumps in the mixture which are too big for your baby then either blend or mash them out with the back of a fork until you have the required consistency.

6. Stir and check the temperature before serving to your baby.

Variations

Also try chick peas or cannellini beans.

Banana Rice

This is another very simple recipe to make, which you can also serve cold as a 'packed lunch'. Later on, when your baby has moved on from weaning, you could also serve it as a hot pudding.

Approximate Cooking Time: 4 minutes

Ingredients

1 small to medium size banana

1 dessertspoon ground rice

125 ml breast milk or infant formula

Method

1. Place the rice and milk in a small metal saucepan and stir together.

2. Roughly chop the banana and add it to the pan.

3. Cook over a moderate heat, stirring continuously. When the mixture starts to bubble turn the heat down slightly.

4. Continue to cook until the banana has melted and you have the consistency you require for feeding.

5. Turn the mixture out into a bowl for feeding and allow to cool.

6. Stir and then check the temperature before serving to your baby.

Variations

Try puréed apple, apricot, peach, or nectarine instead of banana.

Introducing New Tastes and Variety

Some of the ingredients in this section are not suitable for babies under 6 months, refer to page 11 and seek advice from your Health Visitor or GP if you are unsure.

Broccoli and Potatoes in Cheese Sauce

A rich sweet dish full of vegetable goodness.

Approximate Cooking Time: 14 minutes

Ingredients

60 g broccoli florets

1 medium sized potato

50 g mild white cheddar cheese

small amount of butter

115 ml full cream milk

Method

1. Peel and wash the potato.

2. Chop it up into small cubes for faster cooking.

3. Place the pieces into a small metal pan and pour in approximately 150 ml of unsalted water. Cover the pan with a lid and leave to cook over a moderate to high heat. Do check the water level occasionally – if the water is all absorbed by the potato

before it is cooked then just add a little more to finish cooking.

4. While the potato is cooking wash the broccoli and chop it up small for faster cooking.

5. Place the broccoli into a small metal pan and pour in approximately 150 ml of plain unsalted water. Cover the pan with a lid and leave to cook over a moderate to high heat. Do check the water level occasionally – if the water is all absorbed by the broccoli before it is cooked then just add a little more to finish cooking.

6. Meanwhile grate the cheese.

7. Test the potatoes with a knife – they should be very soft and all the water will have evaporated.

8. Turn the heat down as low as possible and add the cheese to melt over the hot potato by mashing them together with a potato masher.

9. Once the cheese has melted, gradually add the milk and continue mashing with the back of a fork or potato masher.

10. Test the broccoli with a knife – it should be very soft.

11. Place the butter in the pan with the broccoli and mash them together with a potato masher.

12. Now mix the contents of both saucepans together

and continue mashing until you have the consistency you require.

13. Turn out into a bowl for feeding and allow to cool.

14. Stir and then check the temperature before feeding to your baby.

Egg Custard

This recipe is so simple and easy to make and you can add soft fruit to it to make it more interesting for an older baby.

Approximate Cooking Time: 4 minutes

Ingredients

125 ml full cream milk

1 medium size egg

Method

1. Heat the milk in small metal saucepan over a moderate heat. It will not take long to warm through so keep a close eye on it.

2. Meanwhile beat the egg in a cup until you have a uniform colour.

3. Just as the milk is coming close to boiling add the

beaten egg, stirring continuously so as not to let the milk boil over.

4. Keep stirring and cook the egg thoroughly, the custard will start to become thick.

5. Once the egg has cooked and you don't think the mixture will thicken any more, turn the custard into a bowl for feeding and allow to cool.

6. You will find the custard continues to thicken as it cools down.

7. Stir and then check the temperature before feeding any hot food to your baby.

Tarragon Chicken

Tarragon and chicken always work well together and this is a very tasty recipe. You can make the tarragon flavour as mild or as strong as you like. If you are using dried tarragon rather than fresh, place some chopped leaves into boiling water to soften while the chicken is cooking and use to season the dish. Serve the dish with mashed vegetables, French beans or spinach.

Approximate cooking time: 9 minutes

Ingredients

55 g fresh chicken breast, skinned and boned

1 large pinch chopped tarragon leaves

115 g full cream milk

1 slice thick white bread

Method

1. Slice the chicken as small as you can for quicker cooking.

2. Place in a small metal saucepan and pour in approximately 150 ml of unsalted water.

3. Add the tarragon, dried or fresh and cover the pan with a lid and bring to the boil over a moderate to high heat. Do check the water level occasionally, if the water is all absorbed by the chicken before it is cooked then just add a little more to finish cooking.

4. Meanwhile cut the crusts off the slice of bread and tear it into small pieces – older infants may like to chew on the bread crusts while they're waiting for dinner!

5. The chicken must be thoroughly cooked (about 5 minutes).

6. Test by cutting into one of the bigger pieces. The chicken must be a uniform white colour.

7. Once the chicken is cooked, turn it out onto a clean chopping board and shred it until it's small enough for your baby to eat – use a knife and fork if it is still too hot to touch. It should crumble easily.

8. Place all the ingredients together into a small saucepan and stir continuously over a moderate heat.

9. The bread should gradually absorb all the milk, but turn the heat down if the milk starts to boil before you reach that stage.

10. The mixture should become thick and gloopy. Add more milk if you need a thinner texture or add more bread if you need a thicker, drier texture.

11. Turn the mixture into a bowl for feeding and allow to cool.

12. Stir and then check the temperature before feeding to your baby.

Variations

Try the same method with turkey breast or ham with thyme. If your baby likes the flavour of herbs, and you want to add more at the final stage of cooking as a seasoning, then pre-soak some herbs in boiling water to soften them first. If you are buying pre-packed or smoked ham always avoid packs with added salt which may have been used in processing the meat.

Cheese and Tomato with Macaroni

Macaroni cheese is a popular dish for children and I have added some tomato for extra flavour and texture. I have made the sauce using ground rice for quickness but a traditional sauce made using melted butter, stirring in a little flour and gradually adding the milk, would work just as well but it would take a little longer to prepare. To speed up the cooking time place the dry, uncooked macaroni in a freezer bag and, holding the edges closed, smash into smaller pieces using a rolling pin.

Approximate Cooking Time: 11 minutes

Ingredients

55 g mild white cheddar cheese

1 large beef tomato or 2–3 small ones

85 g full cream milk

1 dessertspoon ground rice

50 g short cut macaroni

Method

1. First start to cook the macaroni in a small metal saucepan in unsalted water on a medium to high heat.

2. Then start to remove the skin from the tomato(es) by pricking them with a sharp knife several times and submerging the tomato in a bowl of boiling water until the skin starts to peel back.

3. Place the tomato(es) under cold running water to cool it down and carefully remove all the skin.

4. Cut the tomato(es) into four quarters and remove any hard green core, then roughly chop into small pieces.

5. Grate the cheese.

6. Put the rice and milk into a small metal saucepan and stir together.

7. Cook until the rice is soft, but don't let the milk boil.

8. Add tomato and cheese to the milk and rice mixture and cook over a moderate heat, stirring continuously.

9. When the cheese has melted and the tomato has completely broken up, turn off the heat.

10. When the macaroni has cooked soft, drain the water and add the cheese and tomato mixture and stir together.

11. Mash the macaroni with a fork or blend it until you have the texture you require.

12. Turn the dish into a bowl for feeding and allow to cool.

13. Stir and check the temperature before serving to your baby.

Variations

You could add herbs or some spring onion to increase or vary the flavour and try experimenting with other cheeses. Avoid the very salty ones such as Feta, Danish Blue and especially processed cheese which contains added salt and additional sodium.

Eggy Bread

With this very easy recipe, if you are going to take the shortcut of beating the egg and milk together in the saucepan, which I do, then do not use a Teflon coated saucepan or you may end up adding Teflon to your baby's meal!

Approximate Cooking Time: 4 minutes

Ingredients

1 medium size egg

125 ml full cream milk

2 slices white bread

Method

1. Cut the crusts off the sliced bread and tear into small chunks.

2. Crack the egg into a small metal saucepan, add the milk and beat together with a fork, until you have an even colour throughout.

3. Add the chunks of bread and place on a moderate heat stirring continuously.

4. The egg should be thoroughly cooked and all the liquid absorbed by the bread. Continue to stir until you have the consistency you need. Turn into a bowl for feeding and allow to cool.

5. Stir and check the temperature before feeding to your baby.

Variations

Brown bread gives a more malty flavour but for younger infants avoid granary, wholemeal or malted bread which may contain hard wheat flakes. Older infants who are learning to chew may like to chew and suck on the bread crusts, but they must be supervised in case of choking.

Parsley Potato Creamed with Fromage Frais

This recipe works well as a cold 'packed lunch' during weaning but you could also use it as a salad by leaving the potato in small cubes, once the baby has moved on from weaning.

Approximate Cooking Time: 15 minutes

Ingredients

1 medium size potato

1–2 tablespoons of fromage frais or natural yoghurt

large pinch fresh parsley

Method

1. Wash and peel the potato.

2. Cut it into small pieces for quicker cooking.

3. Place the potato into a small metal saucepan and pour in approximately 150 ml of unsalted water.

4. Cover the pan with a lid and leave to cook over a moderate to high heat. Do check the water level occasionally – if the water is all absorbed by the potato before it is cooked then just add a little more to finish cooking.

5. Meanwhile wash and finely chop the parsley.

6. Test the potato with a knife – it should be soft.

7. If the potatoes are cooked then mash them with a potato masher, using a little milk if necessary.

8. Add enough fromage frais to achieve the consistency you need for feeding.

9. Mix in the parsley to season.

10. The dish should be cool enough for feeding but always stir and check the temperature before serving to your baby.

Variations

Use chives instead of parsley, but pre-soak them in boiling water before use to soften them. Natural yoghurt works well too if you can't get hold of fromage frais.

Mackerel and Whole Grain Rice

This meal is delicious. The mackerel, an oily fish, is ideal for this type of cooking because it breaks up easily and cooks quickly. You can buy mackerel fillets from most fishmongers, but be careful not to buy the peppered variety by mistake. If you are buying from a supermarket and the mackerel is pre-packed, rather than fresh, you must check for and avoid added salt or other additives. Serve with mashed vegetables – peas would work well with this dish. While oily fish is very good for us all, it is recommended that infants eat no more than two portions of oily fish per week.

Approximate Cooking Time: 15 minutes

Ingredients

55 g fresh or pre-packed mackerel

40 g whole grain rice

125 ml full cream milk

Method

1. First start cooking the rice in a small metal saucepan. Cover with water and cook over a moderate to high heat.

2. Lay the mackerel skin side down on a clean chopping board, pull the meat away from you without breaking the skin and check all the time for any bones which may have escaped the filleting process.

3. Flake the mackerel into smaller pieces; if you do it with your fingers then you can make doubly sure there are no bones.

4. Place the flaked mackerel in a small metal saucepan and add the milk.

5. Cook over a moderate heat, stirring all the time.

6. When the mixture starts to bubble, turn the heat down and continue stirring until the mackerel is thoroughly cooked.

7. Once the rice has cooked soft, drain the water and mix the rice with the mackerel, mash with a fork or blend until you have the texture you require.

8. Turn the mixture into a bowl for feeding and allow to cool.

9. Stir and check the temperature before serving to your baby.

Variations

Salmon works well too, as do canned fish like tuna, pilchards or sardines. If you are using canned fish use one which is canned in oil or water rather than brine and always check for and avoid added salt. Most labels will also state whether or not any bones have been left in which could be dangerous for your baby.

Butter Beans and Tomato

Beans and pulses in general are a great source of protein, especially if you and your baby are following a vegetarian diet. You can pre-cook your own beans by soaking them overnight and then boiling for at least 30 minutes until soft, or use canned beans as I have done in this recipe. If you choose canned beans, be sure you are buying a product which does not contain added salt. Most varieties will give this information quite clearly on the label, but if in doubt leave it out.

Approximate Cooking Time: 7 minutes

Ingredients

1 large beef tomato or 2–3 small ones

85 g cooked or canned butter beans

1 tablespoon unsalted water

large pinch ground basil, or dried basil soaked in a
little water

Method

1. First start to remove the tomato skins by pricking the skin with a sharp knife several times and submerging them in a bowl of boiling water until the skin starts to peel back.

2. Run the tomato under cold running water to cool it down and carefully remove all the skin.

3. Cut the tomato into four quarters and remove any hard green core, then roughly chop into small pieces.

4. Wash the beans and discard any water.

5. Place them in a small metal saucepan with the water and tomato and start to cook over a moderate heat.

6. Add the basil, or basil and water, and stir.

7. Once the mixture starts to bubble turn the heat down and stir continuously until the beans are soft enough to break up easily.

8. Turn the mixture out into a bowl for feeding and allow to cool.

9. Remove any remaining bean skins and if there are still lumps in the mixture which are too big for your baby then either blend with a handheld blender or mash them out with the back of a fork.

10. Stir and check the temperature before serving to your baby.

Variations

Try chick peas with coriander instead of basil or lentils
with a little unsalted butter and thyme, or cannellini
beans with a little oregano and basil.

Chicken and Leek Savoury Pudding

A very creamy dish, although the flavours are light. A very tasty introduction to more complex flavours and herbs.

Approximate Cooking Time: 15 minutes

Ingredients

55 g chicken breast, skinned and boned

30 g whole grain rice

40 g leek

125 ml full cream milk

large pinch dried/fresh sage

Method

1. Place the rice in a small saucepan with approximately 150 ml of unsalted water and cook it over a moderate to high heat until it is soft.

2. Slice the chicken as small as you can for quicker cooking.

3. Place in a small metal saucepan and pour in approximately 150 ml of unsalted water.

4. Add the sage, dried or fresh, and cover the pan with a lid and bring to the boil over a moderate to high heat. Do check the water level occasionally – if the water is all absorbed by the chicken before it is cooked then just add a little more to finish cooking.

5. Meanwhile wash the leek thoroughly and chop it as small as you can.

6. The chicken must be thoroughly cooked (about 5 minutes).

7. Test by cutting into one of the bigger pieces. The chicken must be a uniform white colour.

8. Once the chicken is cooked, turn it out onto a clean chopping board and shred it until it's small enough for your baby to eat – use a knife and fork if it is still too hot to touch – it should crumble easily.

9. Now put the chicken cooked in sage and the leek back into the saucepan together with the milk and cook over a moderate heat until the leek is soft.

10. Once the rice is cooked add it to the chicken and leek mix, and stir together until it is a lovely creamy texture – if it gets too dry then add a little more milk and stir until the milk is cooked through.

11. Turn out into a bowl for feeding and allow to cool.

12. Stir and then check the temperature before feeding to your baby.

Scrambled Egg with Mushy Peas

This is another very simple dish to make which can be used at different stages of weaning depending on the texture. It can be served with toasted fingers of bread or bread sticks. Remember that frozen peas are just as good as fresh and are very convenient to use.

Approximate Cooking Time: 8 minutes

Ingredients

1 medium size egg

85 g fresh or frozen peas

50 ml full cream milk

Method

1. Wash the peas then put them into a small metal saucepan with approximately 150 ml of unsalted water.

2. Cover the pan with a lid and leave to cook over a moderate to high heat. Do check the water level

occasionally – if the water is all absorbed by the peas before they are cooked then just add a little more to finish cooking.

3. Meanwhile beat the egg and milk together in another small metal pan until the mixture is a uniform colour.

4. Test the peas to make sure they have cooked and once they are cooked add them to the egg mix.

5. Cook the peas and egg mix over a moderate heat stirring continuously.

6. Once the eggs have scrambled and are thoroughly cooked turn the mixture into a bowl and mash the peas with the back of a fork or blend the mixture until you have the consistency you need for feeding.

7. Turn the mixture out into a bowl for feeding and allow to cool.

8. Remove any pea skins which have not cooked and will not mash.

9. Stir and check the temperature before serving to your baby.

Variations

French beans also work well, but remember to mash them well.

Creamed Potato with Cheese

I like this dish because it is very similar to a dish you might eat yourself, in this case a Baked Potato with Cheese, gradually introducing your baby to your own food. It has been adapted to avoid serving the skin and to provide the texture you need for feeding your baby.

Approximate Cooking Time: 15 minutes

Ingredients

1 medium size potato

50 ml full cream milk (amount may vary depending on consistency)

55 g mild white cheddar cheese

Method

1. Wash and peel the potato.

2. Chop it into small pieces for quicker cooking and place them into a small metal saucepan. Pour in approximately 150 ml of unsalted water.

3. Cover the pan with a lid and leave to cook over a moderate to high heat. Do check the water level occasionally – if the water is all absorbed by the potato before it is cooked then just add a little more to finish cooking.

4. Meanwhile grate the cheese.

5. Test the potatoes with a knife, they should be soft.

6. Turn the heat down as low as possible and add the cheese to melt over the hot potato by mashing them together with a potato masher.

7. Once the cheese has melted, gradually add the milk and continue mashing with the back of a fork or blend the mixture until you have the consistency you need for feeding.

8. Place the mixture into a bowl and allow to cool.

9. Stir and check the temperature before serving to your baby.

Variations

Try other baked potato fillings like baked beans or tuna fish, but leave out the mayonnaise!

Cannellini Beans with Brussels Sprouts

Green leaves served with bacon is a classic combination, however, as bacon does contain added salt, I have chosen cannellini beans instead, which have a wonderful ham-like flavour. Although most of us try to avoid soggy Brussels sprouts around Christmas time, it is the fact that sprouts break up so quickly that make them ideal for baby food. You could serve this dish with mashed potato or boiled whole grain rice as it is a high fibre dish and one of these will help balance out the fibre you will be feeding to your baby.

Approximate Cooking Time: 14 minutes

Ingredients

70 g cooked or canned cannellini beans

70 g Brussels sprouts

130 ml tomato juice, straight from a carton or drained from a can of tomatoes

Method

1. Clean the sprouts and remove the old outside leaves.

2. Cut the sprouts in quarters and place into a small metal saucepan with approximately 150 ml of unsalted water.

3. Cover the pan with a lid and leave to cook over a moderate to high heat. Do check the water level occasionally – if the water is all absorbed by the sprouts before they are cooked then just add a little more to finish cooking.

4. Meanwhile wash the beans and discard the water.

5. Place the beans and the tomato juice in a small saucepan and cook over a moderate heat until the beans are soft.

6. Add the soft cooked sprouts to the beans and stir well.

7. Turn the mixture into a bowl and allow to cool.

8. If there are still lumps in the mixture which are too big for your baby then either blend or mash them out with the back of a fork until you have the consistency you need for feeding.

9. Stir and check the temperature before serving to your baby.

Variations

Try finely shredded cabbage. This may need blending before you serve, depending on the age of the baby. Spinach will also work very well.

Cauliflower Cheese

This recipe tastes just like the version you eat yourself. I have made the sauce using ground rice for quickness but a traditional sauce made using melted butter, stirring in a little flour and gradually adding the milk, would work just as well, though it would take a little longer to prepare.

Approximate cooking time: 12 minutes

Ingredients

85 g mild white cheddar cheese

125 ml full cream milk

55 g cauliflower

1 dessertspoon ground rice

Method

1. Wash and chop the cauliflower into small pieces for faster cooking.

2. Place into a small metal pan, pour in approximately 150 ml of plain unsalted water.

3. Cover the pan with a lid and leave to cook over a moderate to high heat. Do check the water level occasionally – if the water is all absorbed by the cauliflower before it is cooked then just add a little more to finish cooking.

4. Meanwhile grate the cheese.

5. When the cauliflower is soft enough to break apart with the side of a fork, chop it into very small dice.

6. Place the ground rice and milk into a small metal saucepan and stir them together.

7. Place over a moderate heat and add the cheese to melt, stirring continuously.

8. When the mixture starts to thicken, add the chopped cauliflower and continue to stir until the sauce is as thick as you require, be careful not to let the sauce boil and burn.

9. Turn the mixture out into a bowl for feeding and allow to cool.

10. If there are still lumps in the mixture which are too big for your baby then either blend or mash them out with the back of a fork.

11. Stir and then check the temperature before serving to your baby.

Variations

Try experimenting with other cheeses, but be careful not to choose ones which are too salty e.g. Feta, Danish Blue or Processed Cheese which contains added sodium. If you are in any doubt, then ask for advice before you buy. A tasty alternative to cauliflower is broccoli.

Potato with Chopped Egg

This is a classic combination of foods which you will find very versatile. Serve it with a chopped green leaf like spinach or Brussels sprouts.

Approximate cooking time: 15 minutes

Ingredients

1 medium size potato (about 115 g peeled, washed potato)

1 medium egg

30 ml full cream milk

Method

1. Wash and peel the potato and chop it into small cubes for quicker cooking.

2. Place in a small metal saucepan and pour in approximately 150 ml of unsalted water.

3. Cover the pan with a lid and leave to cook over a moderate to high heat. Do check the water level occasionally – if the water is all absorbed by the potato before it is cooked then just add a little more to finish cooking.

4. Meanwhile hard boil the egg in another small pan. This time it is essential that the water is boiling before you add the egg.

5. Once the egg is hard (about 5–6 minutes), take the pan off the heat, put it in the sink and run some cold water into the pan.

6. Once the egg is cool enough to touch, remove the shell, and rinse the egg under cold running water to wash away any small pieces of shell which could be dangerous to the baby.

7. Chop the egg into small pieces and leave to cool.

8. When the potato is cooked soft, add the chopped egg and mash them up together with the milk, using a potato masher.

9. Turn the mixture out into a bowl for feeding and allow to cool.

10. If there are still lumps in the mixture which are too big for your baby then either blend or mash them out with the back of a fork, use some extra milk if you need a smoother texture.

11. Stir, then check the temperature before serving to your baby.

Variations

Sweet potato is very colourful and quick and easy to cook, as it is much softer than other potatoes.

Broccoli and Whole Grain Rice

Broccoli is especially good for you and your baby and is easy to use when you are in a hurry because it cooks soft so quickly.

Approximate Cooking Time: 15 minutes

Ingredients

85 g broccoli

40 g whole grain rice

125 ml full cream milk

Method

1. Place the rice in a small saucepan with approximately 150 ml of unsalted water and cook it over a moderate to high heat until it is soft.

2. Wash the broccoli.

3. Thinly slice it and place into a small metal saucepan with the milk and cook over a moderate heat, taking care not to let the milk boil.

4. Test the broccoli to make sure it is cooked and once it is soft, mash it into the milk with the back of a fork.

5. Add the broccoli and milk mixture to the rice and stir well.

6. Turn the mixture into a bowl for feeding and allow to cool.

7. If there are still lumps in the mixture which are too big for your baby then either blend or mash them out with the back of a fork until you have the consistency you need for feeding.

8. Stir and check the temperature before serving to your baby.

Variations

Try using chopped green beans or peas.

Ground Beef with Herbs and Potato or Pasta

This recipe idea is very versatile and you can experiment with different meats and herbs, to introduce your baby to different tastes and textures. With potato you have the basis for your own version of cottage pie and with pasta you have the basis for Bolognese, you are simply paring the dish right down until your baby becomes accustomed to the taste and then you can build it back up again, adding in the additional vegetables and ingredients, to a dish which is a family favourite and which, with some minor adjustments, your baby will be able to eat with the family. To store the meat for this type of cooking, weigh some meat into little 2 oz parcels and keep in the freezer. To speed up the cooking time for pasta place the dry, uncooked pasta in a freezer bag and, holding the edges closed, smash into smaller pieces using a rolling pin.

Serve the finished dish with mashed vegetables like carrots or peas.

Approximate Cooking Time: 15 minutes

Ingredients

55 g minced/ground beef

1 medium potato or 2 oz pasta of your choice

30 g butter

large pinch basil

large pinch oregano

2 or 3 tablespoons full cream milk

Method

1. Peel and wash the potato.

2. Chop it up into small cubes and place in a small metal saucepan. Pour in approximately 150 ml of unsalted water.

3. Cover the pan with a lid and leave to cook over a moderate to high heat. Do check the water level occasionally, if the water is all absorbed by the potato before it is cooked then just add a little more to finish cooking.

4. Meanwhile melt the butter in another metal pan over a low heat, being very careful not to let it foam or brown.

5. Add the herbs to the butter and gently cook them for about 2 minutes. Do not fry the herbs hard or they may develop a bitter taste.

6. Make sure the meat has been minced small enough for your baby to eat. If not then finely chop it.

7. Add the meat to the herb butter and gently cook the meat until it is completely browned.

8. Check that the potatoes are cooked and once they are soft, add them to the meat and herbs and

mash them up together with the milk using a potato masher.

9. Add more milk if you need a smoother consistency. Then either mash out any remaining lumps with the back of a fork or blend the mixture until you have the required consistency.

10. Turn the mixture out into a bowl for feeding and allow to cool.

11. Stir and then check the temperature before feeding to your baby.

Variations

Experiment with other combinations of meat and herbs, like minced pork with ground rosemary or minced chicken with tarragon or ground sage.

Noodles with Sweet Pepper and Egg

As the name suggests, sweet pepper is a lovely sweet fruit – which we often use as a vegetable. Babies and children will like the combination of fresh light tastes once they have moved on to a varied diet of solid foods.

Approximate Cooking Time: 12 minutes

Ingredients

55 g yellow or red pepper

30 g red onion or spring onion

40 g noodles, thick or thin, egg or plain, it doesn't matter

1 egg

1 clove garlic

splash of olive oil

Method

1. Break the noodles with your hands into small enough pieces for your baby to eat.

2. Place the noodles in a small metal saucepan.

3. Pour approximately 150 ml of unsalted water over the noodles and cook over a high heat until soft.

4. Peel and trim the onion and chop it as fine as you can.

5. Place a splash of olive oil into a small metal

saucepan with the onion and cook over a medium heat until soft but not browned.

6. Peel the garlic clove and chop very fine or crush it into the onion.

7. Wash the pepper and remove any seeds or stalk and chop as fine as you can.

8. Add the pepper to the onion and cook until soft enough for your baby to eat.

9. Beat the egg into a uniform colour and add to the vegetables.

10. Stir the egg and vegetable mix until all the egg is completely cooked through, be careful not to let the egg stick to the bottom of the pan.

11. Drain the noodles if there is any water left and add them to the vegetable mix, stirring well.

12. Mash the mixture with a fork until you have the consistency you require for feeding.

13. Turn the meal out into a bowl for feeding and allow to cool.

14. Stir and then check the temperature before serving to your baby.

Variations

You could try finely chopped courgette or peas instead of sweet pepper. Also try cooking a variety of vegetables

in the same way to combine with pasta as an
alternative to noodles. If you want to experiment with
more exotic flavours try adding a pinch of star anise to
the dish at the start.

Using Soups

If you make your own soups you will find they are a great way to further vary your baby's diet. There are any number of cookery books specialising in ideas for soups but if you cook your own food from fresh ingredients already then you probably have your own favourite recipes to use. Canned and pre-prepared soups may contain added salt and can be very concentrated, so I wouldn't give them to a baby younger than 9–12 months. When you are cooking your own soup add less stock than you normally would for your own taste and don't add any salt at all. Once the soup is ready, minus the salt, take some out for your baby and put it in the fridge or freezer until you are ready for it, you can then go ahead and season the remainder for your own taste.

You may need to blend your baby's portion of soup and if so a handheld blender is a very useful tool to have. Once you have blended or mashed the soup you may find, unless it is very thick, that feeding your baby with soup can be difficult as it tends to get everywhere but in the baby's mouth. So take a slice of white bread and cut the crusts off. Tear it up into small pieces and put them into the warm soup. Mash the bread into the soup and give it a few seconds until the bread soaks up all the liquid. Keep adding bread in this way until you have the consistency you need for feeding and always test the temperature before you give it to your baby. If you have more time you could add a little mashed potato instead of bread to thicken most soup.

Many soups taste equally good hot or cold e.g. Gazpacho, and they will make a great 'packed lunch'.

Preparing Your Own Meals for Your Baby to Eat

Ultimately you want your baby to eat what you eat so you are not always cooking two different meals, one for you and one for the baby, and to encourage a family meal time. However, it is important to note that babies younger than 9 months should not be given pre-prepared adult foods – this includes any bottled, canned or dried 'cook in' type sauces, gravies or gravy browning, batters or snack foods as well as any pre-prepared whole meals. These foods contain too much salt and other added ingredients. So if you are going to feed your baby some of your own meals then only give home-made food. When I use the words 'home-made food' I mean a meal which is made using only fresh or frozen vegetables, meat or fish and other raw ingredients. If you are in any doubt over the suitability of the food for your baby or the age to start preparing your own food for your baby, then you should seek advice from your Health Visitor or doctor and remember that some foods are not suitable for babies under 6 months.

When you are preparing your own home cooking and you want the baby to try some then use less salt and stock during cooking than you normally would. It will be healthier for you too. This includes boiling vegetables or pasta in unsalted water. Once the meal is ready, minus the salt, take some out for your baby and put it in the fridge or freezer until you are ready for it. You can then go ahead and season the remainder for your own taste. You can very quickly build up a stock of frozen meals.

Pasta with home-made sauce works very well as a baby meal because it mashes into a smooth paste. However, once you have blended or mashed some other meals you may find they are too runny to feed easily to your baby. You can either add bread in the same way suggested for soups or add a cooked mashed potato. However, if you are feeding a younger baby and you are in a hurry, you could use ground rice as detailed below. This method works best for home-made sauces like mild curries or casserole sauces. The addition of milk dilutes the taste a little which you may find your baby prefers until he or she gets used to it. Gradually you can add more sauce and less milk. Always give your baby a beaker of water and let them drink as much as they wish during the meal.

Prepare your own home-made sauces or casseroles for your baby using ground rice

Ingredients

Approximately 85 g of entirely home-made sauce with the main meat, fish or vegetable ingredient mashed or blended

1 dessertspoon ground rice (for variations see below)

114 ml full cream milk

Method

1. Blend or mash the home-made sauce until it is as smooth as you require.

2. Mix the sauce and the rice together in a small metal saucepan.

3. Add the milk and cook the mixture over a moderate heat stirring constantly until you have the consistency you require.

4. Turn the mixture out into a bowl for feeding and allow to cool.

5. Stir and then check the temperature before feeding any hot food to your baby.

Variations

Substitute the ground rice with a small cooked potato or a slice of white bread.

Finger Foods

As babies become used to eating solid food, finger foods are a great way of encouraging babies to explore their food as they feel the texture and examine it in minute detail. It also encourages chewing and gives them practice with feeding themselves before they eventually progress onto a spoon. Don't worry if they don't actually eat finger foods so much as wear it the first few times – eventually they will figure out how to put it in their mouths!

Always encourage savoury food like vegetables or fruit. If you offer sweet snacks you may find your baby will want to bypass their meal altogether and go straight to the snacks – this will create difficulties in weaning onto a varied diet. Never leave your baby unattended when they are chewing finger food.

Some suggestions:

Carrot sticks, raw or cooked
Cauliflower or broccoli florets, cooked and cooled
Banana, but not green ones
Apple or melon, peeled and cut into chunks
Crusts of bread, not soda bread
Toast, cooled
Cooked pasta, cooled e.g. pasta shells
Sweet red or yellow pepper, raw, cut into sticks
Quarters of ripe apricot or plum, with the stones removed

Mild cheese cut into cubes

Naan or pitta breads cut into strips

Do remember that some foods are not suitable for
babies under 6 months.

Index